A STROKE
OF THE PEN

A STROKE OF THE PEN

RICK BOZIC

Copyright © 2014 by Rick Bozic.

Library of Congress Control Number: 2014922452
ISBN: Hardcover 978-1-5035-2817-8
Softcover 978-1-5035-2818-5
eBook 978-1-5035-2819-2

All rights reserved. No part of this book may be reproduced or transmitted in any form or by any means, electronic or mechanical, including photocopying, recording, or by any information storage and retrieval system, without permission in writing from the copyright owner.

Any people depicted in stock imagery provided by Thinkstock are models, and such images are being used for illustrative purposes only.
Certain stock imagery © Thinkstock.

This book was printed in the United States of America.

Rev. date: 12/19/2014

To order additional copies of this book, contact:
Xlibris
1-888-795-4274
www.Xlibris.com
Orders@Xlibris.com
701131

CONTENTS

Stuck in the Middle 13
Terror in the Shadows 14
Forever.. 16
Waiting for the Whisper 17
Drug of Choice 18
-Red 19
One Wish, If Only... 20
Whole Again... 21
Accept 22
For Whom the Bell Tolls 23
Farewell to Freedom 24
Locked On 25
My Princess Angel 26
It Is Time 27
Silver Penny 28
Butterflies... 29
Paranoia 30
The Birth of Nothing 31
Death before Life 32
Prophetic Justice 33
The Power of Adoration 34
6.. 35
Portraits of Fire 36
Midnight Dream 37
Prince of Peace 38
Fingers of Death... 39
One Heart Miles Away 40
Hidden Love 41
A Change of Seasons 42
No More 43

My Broken Promise 44
The Wealth of Love 45
Where Have I Gone? 46
Bobby 47
Heaven Sent 48
Filiation Destroyed 49
Oh Please, God, Wake Me 50
Tsunami 51
One Last Time 52
Surrendering Life 53
Lesion of Desire 54
He Has Risen 55
The Indwelling 56
Inches to Nowhere 57
The Last Tear 58
Stages 60
Friends for Life 62
One Chance 63
Love Hurts 64
Two Bodies, One Heart 65
God's Gift to the World 66
-Red II 67
Not Me 68
I Believed 69
Appalling 70
It's My Fault 72
The Bases Are Loaded 73
My Promise to You 74
Ghosts 75
A Ritual 76
My Baby True 77
I Cried 78
The Offspring 79
Success in Failure 80
Delicately Cruel 81
Calculations 82
Contained 83
Take Your Pick 84

Suppression	85
Looking Back	86
Nobody Knows	87
September Son	88
Over and Again	90
Resolution	91
-Red III	92
The Empire	93
Lost Promises	94
52 Pick Up	95
Another World	96
Unattainable	97
Love Is . . .	98
Enlightened	99
Alone Again	100
Titanium Sorrows	101
Unconscious Freedom	102
The Pulse	103
A Reason	104
Torn Ends of Sanity	105
Emotionally Sterile	106
Where Did You Come From?	107
Seven Steps to Freedom	108
Back Again	109
The Wall	110
The Friend I Never Had	111
No Easy Answer	112
Love's Repression	113
A Flower Blossoms	114
Sign of the Times	115
Roll of the Dice	116
Bloodline Cast	117
The Mask	118
Fatal Epidemic	119
Carousel	120
Loneliness	121
Searching	122
Game Over	123

Broken Crutch	124
A Man of War	125
Trilogy	126
Chess	127
The Midnight Run	128
-Red IV	129
What Is	130
Courting the Militia	131
The Call	132
From Behind the Wall	133
Ten Years Gone	134
Slipping Away	135
Universal	136
Where Do I Go?	137
The Battle Rages On	138
Keep the Faith	140
Dream Warrior	141
I'm Coming Home	142
The Regime	143
Spiral Genocide	144
Paradise Lost	145
Breathe	146
Carousel	147
One-Way Street	148
The Day of the Dog	149
Time	150
Mount Fury	151
Borrowed	152
Indifference	153
Tick Tock	154
No Wonder	155
Free Falling	156
Rise of the Fall	157
Left Behind	158
Firestorm	159
Razor's Edge	160
Almost There	161
I Believed	162

The Invisible Architect 163
Real Love..164
Pampered..165
The Game of Love 166
When Was the Last Time? 167
The Looking Glass 168

The inspiration for my book started about seven years ago after I suffered a massive stroke that the doctors were amazed that I even survived. Over the course of the next five years, my body was ravaged by one major illness after another. I lived through heart surgery while being awake after the doctor's inadvertently hit a nerve, which woke me up, and they could not get me back under anesthesia. I had to endure the procedure from start to finish wide awake, and I can attest to the fact there is no greater pain in the world than being awake during heart surgery. I suffered two more strokes, not nearly as powerful but definitely taking its toll on my brain and left side functions. All told, I had six stroke and two minor strokes (am recovering from a stroke now). My brain isn't what it used to be but then whose is?

I found that writing poetry, rhyming in particular, would just come to me. I would grab a pen and paper and sit down and write. If it didn't just flow then I wouldn't write it. For me, poetry comes free flowing and it develops as I write it. If I have to sit down and think of a subject to write about, it becomes forced and unnatural. Poetry should be a mixture of all different emotions and doesn't have to have an answer at the end. It should be thought provoking, edgy, and left for the interpretation of the reader. Since my illness, it opened another area of my brain, which left me to write. It usually takes about four to five minutes to write a poem from start to finish without even knowing what I am going to be writing about.

From somebody who medically shouldn't even be here to now writing a book is truly a miracle, and as long as they keep coming, I will keep writing. To read poetry you must have an open mind and a clear head to truly enjoy it.

My daughter Jordanne was an intricate part of this book process. She helped choose which poems should go in the book and also decided the first ones that should be read and the last ones. So a very special thanks to her as she has been one of my biggest supporters through all the rough times and didn't get the normal childhood she deserved, so thank you so much, baby, for always being there.

Even with a brain injury, you can still use your mind.

Stuck in the Middle

Drifting in and out of consciousness
The cord begins to come undone
Can't you hear me crying?
I fear it has only just begun

Why, is the question without an answer
Justification cannot be found
The early frost adjust to its new domain
Suppressing the heat rising from the ground

As daggers of steel drive deep
The bloodless wound begins to bleed
Inoculated against infection
Delivery of peace can proceed

Airborne from reality
The flight is a bumpy ride
Obsessively calm, the beads of sweat cascade
No longer can it provide

Eluding what is inevitable
How can I comply?
I, cannot live
I, cannot die

Terror in the Shadows

Pausing on the back side of a tree
I turn to see if he has come
The masked predator plunges with a knife
Piercing through my chest, my body feels numb

I struggle to get to my feet
With my hand clutching my wound
I've got to run to protect myself
Or this will all be over soon

He must be lurking in the shadows
Because he's nowhere to be found
Like a stealth bomber on a secret mission
He moves without a sound

The blood is pouring out at a feverish pace
My body is drenched in sweat
I cannot go much further
Safety, I will never get

I collapse on the forest floor
Lying in a pool of red
A chill sweeps across my body
Not much longer until I am dead

Hanging over me
With a bloody knife in his hand
It appears that he is smiling
As he gazes across the land

My final breath approaching
I have to do something quick
As my energy slowly fades
I reach over and grab a stick

With one desperate, defiant move
The blow to his head knocks his mask into a tree
I stare into the eyes of the manmade aggressor
Evil has a face, and it is me

Forever

Will you please look after my child?
To make sure he's all right
He doesn't like to be alone
And he's afraid of the night

Him, you cannot possibly miss
With a smile so warm and inviting
He loves to show off his pictures
And letters he is writing

His laughter can fill a room
His poise is beyond his years
He is compassionate about everything
But I worry about his fears

Don't leave him by himself
Without people, he is lonely
His mere presence is priceless
He is the one and only

Treasure his natural gift
Do not let it go to waste
Take a drink of his vitality
Born with the sweetest taste

Waiting for the Whisper

The lingering smell is pungent,
The odor is acidic and sour
It was once thought of nameless
Giving way to its power

Hypnotized by the pendulum
Drawing a foregone conclusion
Powerful and exquisite sensations
The master of illusion

Rolling thunder precedes the flame
The fingers from within the shroud
Electrifying dance to an unruly beat
Shrieking instinctively out loud

Gasping for air that somewhere exists
Struggling to drink from the bottle off tomorrow
Pain and pleasure filter through the sides
Waiting for the screams of sorrow

Shhhh, if you listen real closely
Eventually the answer, it will come
It's much quieter than a spoken word
And more delicate that a hum

Drug of Choice

Looking at my reflection
There's nothing but deception and lack of strength
I need just one more injection
And I'll go to any length

It's the deadliest drug on earth
That kills more people every day
Once you've had a taste of it
You can't live any other way

Once it hits your veins
You feel it head straight for the heart
The appetite is insatiable
And it hits you from start

It leaves you craving more
The desire is always there
You want it every chance you can
Getting it is just a matter of where

There are no dealers
And there's no price to pay
This is the ultimate high
Living with it is the only way

-Red

It's a beautiful thing that cannot be given
The acquisition is something you must earn
Reasoning is a fallacy
For the flameless fire that continues to burn

Hinged on the outer layer
An unborn seed for the theoretic
The flight of desires sparkle
While the benefactor cries for the apologetic

Nary a day or night
Goes without giving proper nutrition
The subconscious is flying solo
Attempting to beak tradition

The cornerstone entombed in a sea of riches
Blossoms under the proper care
Alongside the lonely road
Next to the tree of despair

One Wish, If Only

If I had one wish, if only . . .
I wouldn't chose better health
My illness today made me the man I am
And I can do without the fame or the wealth

One wish, if only
I know exactly what I would chose
It would be absolutely priceless to me
And invaluable to lose

One wish, if only
Wouldn't be some outlandish dream
I would keep it simple and easy
Or that's how it seems

One wish, if only
I know exactly what it would be
I would move the heavens and the earth
To be with you for all eternity

Whole Again

I went to put on my glasses
But only one side was there
I went to mail a letter
But the stamp was only half the fare

I looked into the mirror to get ready
And half the glass was gone
I jumped in my car to leave
I had half a tank, what is wrong?

I went to the bar
To try and settle my fear
I asked for a mug of ale
And instead got half a beer

I went home that night and prayed
And asked what's happening to me?
Then an *angel* came down from heaven
And said I want you to listen closely

It appears that everything in your life
Has suddenly become undone
Hold tightly to the person you know to be your soul mate
And everything will become one

Accept

Your aging heart, a brilliant jewel of fire
Is void of any warmth or light
The sweet nectar of wine that once flowed within
Has been soured from the bite

The perfume on your lips
Speaks words the days will never hear
Crying tears of perspiration,
Sorrow is the gateway to fear

Does the world bow to an empty throne
Or is it all a passing hope
Executing judgment in haste
Embraces condemnation with a grope

Look upon the breath of pestilence
That brought forth you, my wife
Do not attempt to save me from death
Instead, save me from life

For Whom the Bell Tolls

Love is declared in death,
The heart, a stream of water
Idle betrayal from the son
Captured from the arms of the daughter

Pity to the orphaned
Whose heritage is lost forever
Take refuge in the contempt
Fight you until, never

Their hunger urges them
Sacrificing them to the sword
Bare yourself and prosper
Do it on your own accord

Shedding innocent blood
Fills the veins with bile
Put the shoes on and walk a day
Put them on and walk a mile

Farewell to Freedom

Exasperated by the never-ending search
One without a beginning or an end
I was sent on a mission of false pretexts
Because they knew the answer I could not send

On my steed,
I rode off into the night
The quest of impossibility was there
It was just out of sight

The king and his court marveled
At the willingness of my desire
As I left the palace they laughed
Deep down they didn't know I lost the fire

I forced myself to do the king's bidding
Although what he wanted couldn't be won
I could not defy his majesty
After all, I was his only son

I was instructed not to come back
Until the search was complete
I rode off into the sunset
So that no longer next to the king was my seat

Locked On

My love for you is a gift
It's something you never have to earn
I give it to you wholly and unconditionally
And at no point should you ever show concern

The moment our eyes locked on
We could see deep into each others soul
Our eyes can talk forever
While our hearts meld and become whole

It's like the world has stopped
And the heaven's left us room to explore
But our love has a voracious appetite
With the cravings leaving us hungry for more

It's not just an amazing friendship
And how I want you to know all there is about me
It's about the instant connection we made
When our eyes locked on it was inevitable
that we were meant to be

My *Princess Angel*

You were my *Princess Angel*
Long before I knew you existed
You were everything I wasn't looking for
And your love could not be resisted

I had dreams of you
Before we ever met
You filled my every desire
And there was nothing left

I tried not to love you
But fate had another plan
You were my polar opposite
And now I'm your loving man

My love for you knows no boundaries
As you now own the majority of my heart
I give you all that I have
And I did right from the start

Your beauty inside
Hcs made you more attractive on the out
But when love starts from within
That's what true love is all about

It *Is* Time

It's time to unleash the mayhem
Longing to finally be freed
Blasting the frozen tundra with a rein of fire
The apocalypse set forth will succeed

There's no place to hide
When destruction awaits around every bend
Suicide mixed with murder
Makes for an intriguing blend

Pleas of forgiveness echo
As the cries of mercy create laughter
Wandering through the streets alone
Disintegration of unity is what it's after

The harvest of souls begin to accumulate
Gone is the novelty of being alive
The sea of red flows freely
Preparing for the allowed to arrive

Tears of acid strip the city
Consuming all forms of life
The threshold to apprehension is shattered,
Vanished with one thrust of the knife

Silver Penny

I scream but nothing comes out
I cry without any tears to shed
My thirst is unquenchable
And my hunger cannot be fed

Dripping blood from an empty vein
With broken bones that won't heal
Laughter remains subdued
The pain I can no longer feel

Music that once filled my life
Has fallen upon deaf ears
Concealing was does not exist
Behind the corridor of mirrors

Don't worry about me
I always manage somehow
The sunny skies give way
For the day of lightning is now

Butterflies

They dance through the air
With no pattern or design
Their bodies float with the wind
And their flight has no rhyme

They also flutter from deep inside
Creating all sorts of sensations
It's the feelings of love
Causing elevated elations

The longer the butterfly lives
The stronger he binds to his mate
The butterfly has no predetermined course
He leaves it in the hands of fate

The butterfly moves in
To where he finds a place to hide
And settles upon emptiness he feels
So that new love can open wide

When you find that true love
You will know it's real
Because that unguided butterfly
Will come out and teach you how to feel

Paranoia

As the horizon turns a sea of orange
The ominous night begins to linger
When from the hazy sky above
Came a wrinkled, outstretched finger

A whirlwind of ice and cold
Blasted from the finger within
There was nowhere to hide from the mayhem
As an unforetold storm was set to begin

The ground pounded like thunder
As the finger gave a gentle flicker
A dense fog rolled through the plains
And the air became thicker

An eruption of unforeseen forces collided
As the ground started to split in two
The finger seemed to be fixated
Like it enjoyed breaking things meant for you

It was sent here to deny
All of those precious moments in time
He was here to claim it all
And declare that everything is mine

The Birth of Nothing

Chiseling out an existence
Of a form that never existed
Forged from a chilling memory
On a life that couldn't be resisted

Stitched from old thread
That was tossed like yesterday's trash
Woven with little intricacy
One spark and it would turn to ash

The foul stench of rotting soil
Emanates through the core
The procedure was meticulously done
While the guardians protect the door

Corrupting the creation
Their morals were unjust and misguided
They planned their instauration
And everything needed was left provided

The immortal being took pity
As one by one the creators met their demise
They had no idea what they had constructed
And now they have to suffer their own demise

Death before Life

The screams echo in his head
As tears of blood roll down his cheek
Gasping for air that no longer exists
The faceless statues around him start to speak

Whispers are all he hears
As the struggles for life is all that remain
They all come to marvel in this joy
So the witnesses could bless his pain

One by one they passed
In a haze all he saw was a grin
Nameless and faceless they chuckled
As the real pain was yet to begin

Choking on something that wasn't there
Something that truly never existed
The scent of sorrow brought laughter
As that tear of blood could no longer be resisted

Hesitating to drift away
To dream of a time that never was
The faceless were his only reason
They gave him just cause

Prophetic Justice

Hailstorms of fire rain down the creation
As the crowd gathers to applause its demise
It has been decades in the making
Leaving but a few bystanders in surprise

Stripped down to its base
A crumbled ruin of rubble is all that remains
Making room for a new structure
So that nothing will be the same

The heaven's bellowed out
That the creation was not meant to be
Lightning bolts incinerated the rubble
And burned the eyes of all those there to see

There will be a chosen one
Yet to stake her claim
She will be the only one
Who will not be harmed, not be maimed

The dust from the rubble floated
Gently blew in the summer wind
Those who came to mock the creation
Those are marked with sin

The Power of Adoration

Crushed bones from a sea of green
And limbs ripped of a vice of black
Committed to a haunted sanctuary
It's too late to turn back

The drum beats in the distance
Where the butterflies used to dance
The white picket fence stands flawless
Now nobody can catch a glance

Released from the shackles
Begging to be let back in
The clock ticks forward
And the calendar moves to where it began

A fracture in the sky
Two worlds start to emerge
Time to make a decision
On which life to purge

6

The longer I'm away from you
The more my love grows
It takes all I have
Just so that nobody knows

I hide my true feelings
From a wall I started to rebuild
Nobody is allowed entrance
My heart is not able to be filled

I gave it my all
When love burned me at every chance
It's time for me to turn the tables
And spurn loves every advance

You can only try so much
Before the reality hits home
Love isn't meant for everybody
And somebody has to live alone

I'm prepared for a life of solitude
Holding my friends at bay
Love doesn't want me happy
And being alone is where I'm prepared to stay

Portraits of Fire

I want to touch the light of darkness
To enter from inside
Why don't you come join me?
And from reality we shall hide

A rush of innocence
Persuades my empty head
Off the beaten path I reign
I cannot see what others have said

I close my eyes and wave to you
Declaring one last good-bye
I can't live this way any longer
Please don't you cry?

I'm not afraid any more
The fear has been driven out
I hold you close in victory
Yielding to the soldiers of doubt

Take a step back and watch me breathe
For your hunger I will feed
Life, it seems to fade away
Protecting the birth of the unborn seed

Midnight Dream

Dying is a slow process
When death has already started
The walking dead roam patiently
For their time to be departed

Embrace the termination of life
Which could take place years prior
Know that you have reached the pinnacle
And you cannot possibly go any higher

Each breath is a torture
An act of needless and senseless greed
Accept what you know to be true
That death fulfills a need

To realize the day of the dog lives forever
Is to know your place in the scheme
The world lives in the blink of an eye
And dies in a midnight dream

Prince of Peace

You tell me you only want to be friends
That I'm forced to repress my feelings for you
You are able to live as though nothing has happened
When my love is so right, so true

But every time we see each other
Those flames are re-ignited so intense
We can't keep ourselves apart from each other
No matter how high they build the fence

Once our eyes lock on
It's as if there's never a spoken word needed
Our hearts, our souls bond as one
And true love has never been mistreated

We can't just be friends
Because it takes but only one look
Then love rises to the top
And it's like a romance right from a book

Call it chemistry, fate, or destiny
But it has been sent by the *angels* above
Two people sharing the same heart
Can only be called true love

Fingers of Death

Tearing through the stomach
The razors separate flesh from bone
Pain has become the anesthesia
Fear has been left all alone

The veins are plucked one by one
Leaving a trail of bright red on the floor
The nerves are severed in half
As the beads of sweat begin to pour

The screams as it penetrates the skull echo
As spattered fragments of bone decorate the wall
The vocal cords are reduced to ashes
Silence shall become the new mating call

Leaving just a memory
A shell of what once used to thrive
Corpses stand to salute the flag
Remembering how it felt to be alive

One Heart Miles Away

As I lay here in bed
I gaze deeply at the picture I have of you
Your smile, your eyes, your face
Tell a story of love so true

I never go to bed alone
As long as I know you are near
All I have to do is turn on my phone or open my computer
And it's as if you are here

I long for the day
When I can hold your body next to mine
And I can gently caress you
And show you that everything will be fine

Our souls are bonded by a lock
For which there is no key
Our love is meant to be everlasting
And without you I don't know where I'd be

Hidden Love

I've waited a lifetime for something
I never knew I missed
It took me that long
And a few girls that I kissed

I never saw you as an equal
You always deserved better than I could ever give
Here you were out experiencing life
While I fighting just to live

We never got to experience the ups and downs
Of the day-to-day living
But my love for you is eternal
And all I can do is keep on giving

My shoulders are strong
And have been known to carry the weight of the world
But are soft enough to hold you tight
And my chest is wide enough for you to tightly cuddle up and curl

A Change of Seasons

Brothers in arms
We'll fight to the end
Against the forces of misrepresentation
Who strive to make amends

The bile that flows
Deep from within
Conceals the identity
Of the devil's origin

All is not fair in this war
A price has to be paid
Boundaries are non-existent
The sanctuary they are trying to invade

The appetite for destruction
Crushes all rationale
Orphaned memories slide into the hidden
The indelible scars reshape their morale

Contaminated ideals
Perplexing and misaligned
Soothes the merciless oppressor
Who can no longer be confined

No More

To owe the world one's life
Is a terrible price to pay
Sometimes concessions have to be given
To ensure life won't go astray

Nobody will ever forget,
Time will not allow
Forgiveness is a treasured luxury
That will not be used right now

The end of time will bear the scars
From the man who created it in error
His name is to be forgotten
To show nobody cares

To remember is to hate
And hate just fuels the fire
Watching him live is a sin
For his death will only inspire

My Broken Promise

I made myself a promise
One I thought I'd never forget
I had my heart broken many times before
And through my walls nobody would get

My guard was always up
Because the pain was more than I could deal
I would deny myself the chance
As love I didn't want to feel

I turned my back for a moment
And love snuck in the back door
It was more than I ever dreamed
Leaving me wanting more

I got a brief taste of heaven
And all of her desires
But my heart fell to pieces
Left in the embers of a smoldering fire

I cannot do this again
The walls are harder to build
I am left with an emptiness inside
That simply can no longer be filled

The Wealth of Love

I do not own a home
Nor do I have vast wealth
Most of my clothes are outdated
And the only thing going for me is my health

The only thing I can give you
Is a gift like no other
It's a love so deep and strong
You're going to feel emotions that you couldn't from another

Your needs will always come first
And your beautiful smile is all I want to see
I just want to hold you close
And gaze into your eyes for all eternity

My love is like an open book
Where secrets are never kept
Only a lifetime of surprises for my *angel*
And a shoulder for you when you've wept

I will cherish you and adore you
And proudly display our love for the world to see
We are branded from the heavens above
And no longer can we let things just be

Where Have I Gone?

I stop to look into the mirror
But the face I cannot see
I step to look closer
And I cannot even see me

I step outside in hot summer sun
And my shadow hides around the corner
I think I'm losing my sanity
As my shadow latches on to another owner

I turn to look back
And from my house I'm suddenly gone
I shake my head in disbelief
Because something must be wrong

Everything I believed was true
Has shaken me to the core
My day has just begun
I know there's going to be more

I cannot give in to this game
Or the chess master at hand
He's the one controlling the board
And he's developed a master plan

Bobby

I went to your funeral
Because I couldn't believe it was true
You were my best friend since birth
There was no way this could be you

I was the one in the hospital
Nearly on my death bed
You talked to me that night
And said, "What's a couple hundred miles for a best friend?"

I couldn't say good-bye to you
After a lifetime of being brothers
We got along better than friends
We got along like no other

Your death hit me hardest of all
And your mom knew I was dying
I couldn't talk to anybody
I couldn't stop from crying

I didn't think I'd get past it
I was lost and didn't know what to do
But then your mom gave me the greatest gift
Your ashes, to help me get through

Heaven Sent

And the horns rang out
To play the most beautiful song
And the skies soon parted
Lead by a dove they knew it was wrong

The cries of those left behind
They anguished her escape by the closed doors
For it was only her to descend
And nobody more

She floated down and caressed the clouds
As she gently pass them by
Her stunning beauty and angelic presence
Was enough that whoever she touched would softly cry

Heaven's gate opened only for a moment
Just long enough for God to send his *princess* on the right angle
She missed her true mark by only a short distance
But on this day, God sent his heavenly *angel*

Filiation Destroyed

Aggravated by the never-ending pain
That has been like a curse to endure
It has inflicted everyone he's come in contact with
And his soul has been tortured for sure

Condemned in a lifeline
That has consumed all with a touch
The demonic entity is starved for redemption
For reasons that add up to much

Nobody can survive the wrath
Once the fiery sights are locked in
Faith and hope offer little resistance
Through the generations when it began

It's not a game of chance
Or skill, luck, or hiding
It's all just a matter of time
As those fiery eyes are biding

There is only one way to stop the curse
And somebody has to be the one
The end has to come near
The family has to be done

Oh Please, God, Wake Me

Oh please, God, wake me
Before it's too late
There is so much I want to say and do
I don't want to have to wait

Looking at you, only seeing me
What does all of this mean?
My life is flashing before me
Falling on an empty screen

I should have seen it coming
But how was I to know
The end came too quickly
I never had the time to grow

One more chance is all I ask
Surely you can comply
You know all the reasons
I don't have to explain why

I'm sorry that tonight
Has made me relive the years
Oh please, God, wake me
Before the falling rocks crumble into tears

Tsunami

Retribution must be administered
For denying the final call
Leaving the decrepit go untreated
Was a unanimous decision by all

How easy it was to besmirch his name
Criticizing his every deed
Using his thoughts to crucify him
Begging for the man to bleed

The past has handicapped the present
Distorting the images of yore
Revived to serve recompense
Never asking, only demanding more

Incensed with the undertaking
The journey toward vindictiveness is swift
Comforting the thoughtless aspirations
In and out of conscious he begins to drift

The slow methodical approach
Has paved the way for a lonely ride
The transition to tranquility will be laborious
On that day when two worlds collide

One Last Time

A puff of red smoke
Precedes a ball of blue flames
An explosion of unheralded magnitude
The innocent it claims

Caught in the midst
Of a project gone awry
The outstretched fingers from hell
Snatch the naked, never knowing why

The heat is so intense
It can turn glass into sand
The bowels of hell open
As death consumes the land

An everlasting fire ravages the earth
And extends into the sky
It has an unquenchable thirst
That will never be satisfied

Surrendering Life

You don't deserve my loyalty
After all the agony I've suffered through
Yet you strive to empty my soul
With a commitment you can't undo

I do not fit in your world,
Decayed and morally corrupt
Your pathetic attempt to keep unity
Has caused the internal volcano to erupt

Your anger flows like lava
Eliminating life in every form
The ashes in the aftermath
Protects you and keeps you warm

I cannot meet your demands
No matter how hard you try
I love you this much
As I stretch out my arms to die

Lesion of Desire

The motive is not yet apparent
It's concealed under the many layers
Separation requires surgical precision
If only for the disobeyers

Handcuffed to a dream
Without a beginning or an end
Hope is nothing more than an empty promise
No matter how well you pretend

The course has been set
Set for the straight and narrow
Idolized by the naysayers
Following the flight of the broken arrow

Tormented by the shattered chain
Heaped in a corner on the floor
The wisdom that was bound with it
Has been released to be found no more

Gone forever are the days
Where tranquility and success roam free
Trapped beneath the golden rainbow
Lies the skeleton that is me

He Has Risen

Consumed by the fire
The combination of oil and water, it clashes
With a renewed vigor he rises
After spending centuries in its ashes

The separation of what is
And what used to be
Marks the dawning of a new beginning
The heinous creation is finally free

The legend of his rise
Has caused a cataclysmic effect
A phantasm he is no more
His existence they cannot protect

Fearing for their safety
As he descends to his throne
Flight from his clutches is futile
When living with the unknown

He has returned to claim
What was once rightfully his
Your immortal soul he will possess
And everything that is

The Indwelling

The abundance of wisdom
Blossomed over time
Turning away the opposition
With a wordless sign

Attacked since youth
By a force with no name
Accepting the rage,
Accepting the shame

Meditating for days
Trying to repent the sins
I embraced the losses
While they proclaimed the wins

The course has run full circle
Back to where it all started
Leaving me fractured and empty
To soothe the broken hearted

Two times lucky,
Three times shy
The part of me that wants to live
Is the part that wants to die

Inches to Nowhere

Don't go looking
For something you don't want to find
Settling down to ease your emotions
Only puts you further behind

Closing your spirit to the premonition
Never watching what you're seeing
Nirvana isn't a state of mind
It's a state of being

It was not a sensible decision
Witnessed through the two way mirror
Being a descendant of the perverse
Your search for eternal life is your career

Hold on to the night
And release the terror of the day
Force yourself to admit nothing
Pretending that everything is okay

Standing alone, inches to nowhere
The best-kept secret dwells within the charm
Visible only to the apparition
Who strives to protect you from all harm

The Last Tear

The crash, my God, the crash
Oh, how I remember it now
Finally a shadow of hope
Will lay this to rest somehow

My eyes slowly open
Light begins to emerge
I gaze upon this lifeless room
With sudden and desperate urge

Confined to this mechanical bed
My body lies in a state of sleep
So many wires and machines all around
Alive, me they are trying to keep

I know it must be terrible
Judging by the care
The pain is so intense
It's more than I can bear

I open my mouth to speak
But whisper is all I can do
I cradle the words tightly to my chest
Hoping to release them soon

My eyes begin to well
As I utter a single moan
I've been abandoned
Left all alone

Please, please don't desert me now
I just want someone to hold me
To keep me close, safe, and warm
Until finally I am free

The door bursts open
And the crowd gathers, all attempting to speak
Huddled, the family cries
As the last tear rolls down my cheek

Stages

Ice crystals dance through the mist
During the early morning of a late autumn day
Where the spicules of frozen water intermingle
With those that have not conformed to their way

The beauty with which these tiny diamonds cascade
To form a sheet of protection for the ground
Is unmistakable to their rarity
As no two alike will ever be found

It's nature's way of protecting herself
From the fury that's yet to come
When she unleashes torrid storms and fierce winds
Leaving nothing undone

Her beauty slowly fades
As the monster rears her ugly head
It's the dawning of a new creation
Awakened from the dead

Fire of blue cascades from her mouth
Her cries piercing and never ending
Her deadly tears are meant for destruction
Anger is what she is sending

Mercy is for the weak
And the weak she seeks to devour
Cold, calculated, and unrelenting
She consumes them by the hour

Her task will never be complete
Her coming will take many forms
Many have been captivated by her alarming beauty,
Beware of the storms

Friends for Life

Friends for life
Don't need to talk every day
But having a friend for life
Is comfort knowing they'll be there to stay

Years may pass
Before your paths may cross
And conversations pick up
Almost right where you left off

Friends for life
Never judge or tell you what to do
They lend a shoulder to lean on
During the tough times you go through

Many secrets are shared
That only you two know about
And laughter brings smiles
When one of them is down and out

Friends for life are rare
And if you find one you'll know
The best advice I can give
Is never let that friend go

One Chance

If you love something don't set it free
And hope that it may or may not come back to you
You grab hold of that love of your life
And you stay beside them; you stick to them like glue

You wake up every morning and and remind them
Of why you love them before getting out of bed
Do one special thing each day for your love
And I guarantee a lifetime you will be wed

We take for granted in life
And just assume all will be fine
But how can you not notice the person next to you
Who on the inside is dying

Remember, a vow is just a guide book
At any time feel free to do more
Or you just might find one day
Your loved one walking out the door

Love Hurts

Love hurts somebody
It's always an inevitable part of life
Love has no favorites
Whether you're a husband or a wife

Sometimes love dies out
And the words are merely spoken
It's been said for so long
It's just said as a token

When was the last time
Your eyes locked in a gaze
And instead of seeing the soul
Now all you see is a haze

Security is the reason why
People hold on so tight
They have just gotten so used to each other
It doesn't matter if they're out of sight

Fear of the unknown
Is why people hide from true love
Even though they received a thousand signs
Straight from the heaven's above

Two Bodies, One Heart

I hurt so bad cannot explain
I opened my heart to you and let you in
For the first time in my life
In love, I thought I could win

You stirred something inside of me
Feelings I never knew existed
Your love for me in return was unexpected
And your charms could not be resisted

I fell for you
Like I never thought love could make me feel
But seeing you, talking to you, watching you
I know that deep down our love is real

Our love wasn't built on a physical touch
But a binding of two souls
When you put our hearts together
Suddenly we become whole

God's Gift to the World

It was on a cool cloudy night
When from the sky came a bright beam of blue
As it glided gracefully from the heavens
The temperatures finally grew

From within this beam so bright
It could only be an *angel* that came from within
She had beautiful darkened hair, delicate lips
Seductive eyes and a well-formed chin

Her nose was dainty
And her brows were sexy and complete
She had all the features of a *princess*
And she had yet a word to speak

When she uttered her first words
It was like the ancient siren singing her beauty
And it was known that this was an *angel*
Sent from heaven to do love's duty

-Red II

It's an incredible feeling,
One that will last forever
Married to the perception
Creating a new endeavor

The union of souls heats up
With undeniable beauty that's always giving
Returned ten times over
Is what keeps it living

Divorced from the reality
And separated in the dreams
Every day is a holiday in the mind
Or so it seems

Wrongfully accused of murder
The dead is still alive
Buried with the treasures
Stolen was the drive

It has a voracious appetite
That always has to be fed
It's a perfect world to live in
When living with the –red

Not Me

It's become too cliché
Vitally profound
An air of importance
It lingers all around

Abdominal constriction
Surely you have felt
A crash landing in an open field
Or a swishing of a belt

A painted bouquet
Or a tiny bronze shoe
Freshly toasted waffles
Are all cliché too

It is not me
So please don't ask me to try
There are many, many others
Stacked in boxes way up high

It's not the only thing
Nothing more about it can be said
If I haven't answered your question
Apparently this, you haven't read

I Believed

I believed in things that used to be,
Once solid foundations, sturdy and complete
Now dismembered and shattered
The rebuilding process is an insurmountable feat

I believed that the future was the key to the past
Opening doors that were nowhere to be found
Shedding light on the unpredictable
Moving through the maze nary a sound

I believed compassion was the answer
To all of life's questions asked
Materializing in shapeless forms
Spiritual guidance has since been masked

I believed that life was too short
Misconfigured and hopelessly misaligned
Reality shifted to an unforeseen level
That cannot be assembled or easily defined

I believed that life was good
And that was the biggest fallacy of all
Everything will always be nothing
And nothing is what I will call

Appalling

You are not worthy of existence
You wretched, maniacal old fool
Guilty as charged on all accounts I say
To hell with the jury pool

This is my court and these are my laws
I render justice as I see fit
You better look at the harsh reality old man
You deserve everything you get

How dare you stand before me
With those sullen, sunken eyes
I am the master of deception, don't you know?
I can see right through your lies

There is no need for you to utter a single word
I can see the truth written on your face
I hereby cast out everything before you
That of which you cannot replace

The guillotine is too good for you
And the rope is much too quick
Or the chair, the needle, or the gun
There is something else I did pick

It's a minor operation of sorts
That I have been performing with optimal success
I have perfected and refined this procedure
That I can accomplish even under duress

You have been getting too close to the truth
And for that, you must die
As the operation unfolds in front of you
You will begin to understand why

Nothing keeps me from my desires
The end always justifies the means
With my kingdom near completion
The applause overrides your screams

It's My Fault

I didn't sleep at all last night
My eyes never shut
Every time I tried to close them
They opened right up

I came to a sad conclusion
That even though you're the one for me
You cannot return the love
The love that was meant to be

I pour my soul to you
Each and every day
I tell you how much I love you
In every possible way

My love for you cannot be returned
And believe me I totally understand
I am the one to blame
For letting true love get out of hand

You love me as a friend
And I will take that love from you
But the one thing I will miss
Is my true love *angel* not feeling like I do

The Bases Are Loaded

Our love is so complex
For outsiders to understand and see
They don't understand how or why
And maybe they should just let us be

Our connection is more than physical
It has a solid base and that's why it's so strong
For us to ignore all the signs that led us here
Surely would be wrong

I have never given my heart so freely
Where I felt so unguarded yet felt so alive
I want to express my love to you
In so many ways, you have given me the drive

I don't know what else I can do
But I know what's all at stake
It's that every time I open my eyes in the morning
It's next to you I want to wake

My Promise to You

I made a promise to you
To love you with every inch of my soul
And by doing that together
Our hearts will become whole

I made a promise to you
That I would never lie or break your trust
But I never said anything about
Dreaming of us filled with love and lust

I made a promise to you
That I would never let you go
Without showing you or surprising you
How much I love you so

I made a promise to you
That family will always and forever come first
My love is strong enough
To get us through the good times and the worst

Ghosts

The nightmares start out different
But the outcome is always the same
It mirrors the existence of reality
There's only one thing left to claim

Brilliant lights illuminate the background
The chase to its capture
Demons with their sorcery impede progress
One step closer to the rapture

Running for an eternity
From the fingers of the children of the doom
The stillness of the night
Hides the shadows in the room

Malice and prejudice own their lot
Next to where fear stakes its claim
The merciless cries surround the haunted
Nothing will ever be the same

The eerie night tries to penetrate
Dig deep to the core
The surface is virtually fossilized
There has to be a door

Fear gives in to the night
And all it represents
Internal screams are muffled
By the smile of discontent

A Ritual

The morticians line up to prepare the cadavers
For their premature eternal rest
The embalming fluid they administer
Like the others, they hope for success

Brand-new hearses wheel the dead
To the temporary facilities at every pass
Then off to the mortuary
Where the bodies begin to amass

Disbursement of the collected members
Those one thought as brave
Are tossed into the vat of insanity,
Buried in a nameless grave

Reincarnation for the dead is plausible
For some it's guaranteed
Until then, their bodiless souls will roam
Waiting to be freed

Exhumation at an alarming rate
For the families who cannot be deceived
Their loved ones need a proper burial
For they have always believed

My Baby True

I look into the depths of your eyes
And it's as if it's a window to your soul
I can read your every thought and desire
Telling me what you need to be whole

You have always been my other half
And the thought of true love scares you to death
Being with the one you love
Is as easy as taking in a breath

We are drawn like magnets
No matter how hard we try
And when the subject of our love comes up
All you can do is cry

Deep down you want to be loved
To have that man to hold you close
We cannot hide the fact that we are meant for each other
And it's a shame nobody knows

I will wait a lifetime
Because my love is real and true
You stole my heart away a long time ago
And it was only meant for you

I Cried

I cried,
When the music stopped playing
Nevermore to sing to the beat
Or keep the body swaying

The sun vanished,
Lost in the haze
Leaving the moon to provide
The life blood for days

I cried,
Knowing I will never see the rain
The other side of sorrow
Vanished in the sheets of pain

Walking through the garden
The sweet aroma no longer lingers
Gone are the delicate jewels
Removed by the corrupt fingers

I cried,
Losing my sight to the deadly disease
Fighting for my senses
If only, if only, please

The Offspring

A propensity for violence
Laboriously feeding the cycle of melancholy stirs
Daydreams of thunder come to life
Illumination of lightning shadows the words

The milky white screen breathes in distortion
Waiting for the transformation to be born
Images so powerful are displayed
Catapulted beyond the norm

In a macabre and dramatic fashion
There came an outpouring of a terrifying quaver nous wail
Corruption manifested deep from within the bowels of tranquility
Turning away at no avail

Bright red droplets of blood trickle down the screen
Tears of acceptance grace the décor
With the temperance of a demonic angel
A basket of black roses is placed on the floor

Success in Failure

Thank you for everything you failed to do
And promises you refused to keep
Thank you for not nursing me back to health
During those nights I couldn't sleep

I realize now that you are incapable
Of any kind of compassion
Living in the world you created
Distributing your love was out of fashion

You opened my eyes to a world I never knew,
Fantasies that made no sense
You gave me more than I realized
After you took away my innocence

Once upon a very long time ago
I mixed love with confusion
I believed every word you spoke
You created quite the illusion

Thank you for opening my eyes
Done without even trying
You cannot pretend any more
With the dry tears you are crying

Delicately Cruel

Walking on the wings of a dream
Separated from the teeth of security
Influenced by the eccentric and daring
Leaving the power of purity

Falling into the path of resentment
Compelled to ignite the vision
An invitation is forthcoming
Creating a most unpopular decision

The epicenter of hell beckons
Collapsing the structure of distress
It's a new brotherhood never visited
Extracted from the reflection of excess

A lonely, tedious journey
Begins with incurable healing
Vehemently denying alleviation
On a falsehood built on feeling

Standing at attention, on display
For the whole world to see
They can't hear what you don't say
As the thoughts of tomorrow are set free

Calculations

Multiply the sorrows
Then divide them by the pleasures
Subtract the days you have hidden
To find out how it measures

The equation is designed
To prove once and for all
That the greatest gift of life
Can be found inside the wall

Contained

You knew it wouldn't happen tonight
You've been left on your own
Love is strong yet I am so weak
Together we are alone

The pain is going to make you feel all right
As you move closer toward the door
No need to huddle in the corner
With the sterile needles laying on the floor

Do your feelings ever let you go
Or do you need an injection of strength
You take me for the fool you are
And you'll go to any length

A push or a shove
Doesn't even matter
With the touch of a dead man
The particles begin to scatter

Can you feel the silence about to break
Next to the keeper of the dead
Buried under the carnage
Lies the words of the unsaid

Take Your Pick

Talk to me about anything
For I will never judge
My love for you is supportive
And I will never budge

You cannot hide from your feelings
Your heart knows what is true
You can try to convince yourself otherwise
But the only one you're fooling is you

To give up on the chance of true love
Might be the only chance you got
Then you could be stuck in a loveless relationship
And there your love will rot

Love is meant to grow
And not be stagnant and untrue
Would you rather be loved and adored
Or sit back and be blue

You have so much to give
You're warm, tender, and soft
True love would grow with you
Instead of having it lost

Suppression

I want you to love me forever
In ways you just don't know
I wish we could be together
So we could experience true love grow

Love has varying degrees
Mostly with a comfort zone
Familiar love is common
Because nobody wants to be alone

I want to show you
What two people who are bonded can do
A love that is returned a million times over
Makes life easier to get through

How proud would you feel
To show off the one you love
We would be like two young birds
Flying around like two morning doves

My love is real, intense, and undying
And with you it could grow by leaps and bounds
Together, with you,
I want to experience all the emotions, sights, and sounds

Looking Back

I stare into your empty eyes
And the gaze you cannot return
The gateway to your soul is gone forever
Lost is the sparkle that will now only burn

You no longer peer in my direction
But choose to look right through
Grasping firmly to your tainted sympathy
The nightly vigil has all been meant for you

Creating a diversion
That begins with the end
You bury your face in the image
Of a mother without a friend

Brought on to impress
And feed your own selfish desires
Trying to fill the void
From the deceptive you have acquired

Change has always been your mainstay
Replenishing your broken devotion
Trying to capture what does not exist
By dictating the stolen emotion

Burdened by a heavy brow
That hangs above a saddened eye of blue
If you stare too long into the abyss
The abyss stares back at you

Nobody Knows

Nobody knows what it's like
To live your life alone
When you finally die
It's like you've never been known

The true meaning of life
Is to find that one who makes you complete
Sometimes you just have to give up
And admit shameful and utter defeat

There is no sorrow
In living life without love
There is nobody to disappoint
And beg for forgiveness from above

Being alone protects yourself
And allows you from ever being hurt
You never have to worry about the walls you built
Or wearing an armor shirt

I would rather be buried in a nameless grave
Where nobody could mourn the day I die
It's better than allowing your heart access
Where every day you want to cry

September Son

Believe in me,

Desire me,

Love me,

Adore me,

Loathe me,

Despise me,

Discourage me,

Kill me,

Remove the oxygen
So life cannot exist
Place your finger on the button
You know you can't resist

Eliminate your second thought
Before the time expires
Chance your options to the melody
Strip the anchor of any desires

Give me what you need
Allowing you to thrive
Size up the competition
Learn to be alive

Fatal existence
Dripping from a drying bag
I love you terminally
From the heart that cannot gag

Over and Again

Honor, truth, and justice
Where did we go wrong?
Faith, hope, and compassion
Where did we go wrong?

Love is but a foreigner
In a land by thy self
Distant memories slowly vanish
Replaced with contempt itself

Searching for a cause
That has no effect
Slight indifferences overwhelm
Leaving nothing to protect

There is no time to disavow
For the collapse of a broken society
Greeting tomorrow before it has arrived
The affliction had spread ever so slightly

It's a flagrant violation
But does anybody even care
I could be right, I could be wrong
But it's a destitute world we wear

Resolution

Using your deceptive beauty
Slashing your way through an empty life
Flaunting those soulful blue eyes,
Sharp as a dagger and deadly as a knife

You forged an existence out of necessity
Tainted to a passion to excel
Trekking a long side the seraphim,
Snickers the bride of hell

Borrowing an emotion
To satisfy the primal need
Delighting in the mortal fantasies
Creates an alteration for the heart that cannot bleed

Thriving on torture without an end
Rains confusion on your unholy pleasure
Caught in the broken web you have spun
The severity of the aftermath cannot be measured

More is all you need
To fulfill the prophecy of the hated
The father waits earnestly for the rise
Of the new world he created

-Red III

Do not resist the urge
The temptationis far too great
Love has long expired
Meeting a timely fate

The heart is missing,
Never answering the call
Nobody cared or believed
And it was not missed at all

Remember the hurricane
How it takes and never gives
Follow the eye to the beginning
To see why it lives

Capture and harness
The power that breathes
Watch as the creation develops
Into a growth that never leaves

The Empire

Wherever life takes you
It's a place you don't want to go
Visiting relatives who have forgotten
And people you'll never know

A picture paints a new world
One stroke at a time
The canvas is your freedom
And the paint is your mind

Caught in the act
Like a thief in the night
Black widows can kill
From love at first bite

You were given a rose,
A hope and a prayer
Then pawned them for paradise
To live on a dare

Lost Promises

To desire is to dream,
Opening doors you cannot see
Touching a cloud that can't be reached
Or chasing rainbows beyond the trees

Anticipation is ecstasy
At the base of the mountain to climb
A novelist in search of the perfect word,
A poet finding the perfect rhyme

The heart will always allow
The promise of adulation
To cast it into the fire
Only adds to the speculation

Roses and carnations are laid
By the body with overwhelming ease
Good-bye to all the imperfections
And the promises you couldn't seize

52 Pick Up

Why don't you just leave
Before you say something I might regret
This passive façade can't endure
And the horror unleashed, you will never forget

The gentle giant is about to transform
Into a beast programmed to kill
Serenity will be crushed
Onto your own free will

The dream of peace
Will turn into a nightmare of terror
Your immortal cries will go unchallenged
Leaving nothing but a prayer

I tried to warn you
But you're too obtuse to see
Impaired by the many misgivings
The price will be paid by me

Another World

It's a world inside of a world
A claim can be made to which there is no other
Where the foul stench of humanity lies in decay
And morbid rituals become your lover

The lonely, the forgotten, the broken hearted all wait
But hope is nothing more than a fleeting thought
This world is a carnivorous beast always on the prowl
Unfortunately it's a beast that can't beat fought

This world is nothing more than a game
To those who choose to play it for fun
Soiled lives, rotting flesh and paranoia
Are all behind when their day is done

It's a forgotten part of society
A testament of virtues taught anew
A place where we can make ourselves feel better
Down at the human zoo

Unattainable

The wicked lie in wait
For the opportunity to devour
Bloodthirsty and malnourished
Stalking their victims from the tower

Solitude is a morsel,
An unfulfilled treat
Purged after consumption
Chilling the heat

Take envy in the violent
Who crush the whole of the spirit
For they do not cower in frustration
Whenever they are near it

There are no halos in hell,
Dreams or desires
Triumph is an artifact
Hidden beneath the fires

A new version installed
From the warm, lying lips
Alone in the tower waiting
For the crack of the whips

Love Is . . .

Like a sunset,
Painted beauty on a sapphire screen
Incapable of being harnessed
Yet always there to be seen

Like a desolate waterfall,
Cascading into an empty pool
Plunging into the deceptive allure
The undercurrents quickly cool

Like the wind,
Calm as it runs its course
It can be fatally captivating
When its life is run full force

Like a burning ember,
Needing nurturing to ignite the flame
Left to smolder unattended
Its life can never be regained

A mythological beast,
A word created in a time of need
Filled with empty promises
Its name is as shallow as its deed

Enlightened

Encrypted messages arrive
For which only my eyes can see
Detailed instructions await inside
That reveal the hidden "we"

Privy to the understanding
Entitlement is the secret power
The intensity lives in the petal
Protecting the heart of the flower

Proceed with caution
And forgive yourself for the loss
Bow your head in abhorrence
Bow down at the foot of the cross

A disparaging comment rejected
Is a concealed compliment received
However fortunate to walk the days
Alone, if you ever believed

Alone Again

You have driven a steak through my heart
For one last final time
You thrive on greed and self-loathing
Thinking that everything is mine

You take without giving
Using your tears as a ploy
I'm tired of being used by you
I'm tired of being your toy

You take my kindness
And twist it to meet your needs
But you're slowly destroying me from the inside
As long as you continue to feed

Women like you take a good man
And force him to build a wall around his heart
Now he trusts nobody because of your deceit
Then he has to go back to the start

You ruined somebody who loved unconditionally,
A free spirit who adored the world
Now a secluded recluse
One who'd rather sit by a fire alone, furled

Titanium Sorrows

If you look forward
You can't escape the past
The evil that has been chasing you
Has you running very fast

The demons inside
Are fighting to get out
They know who you are
And exactly what you're about

The faster you run
And the more you hide
Protects yourself from all
All who want to get inside

It's a place nobody can be
It's been vacated years ago
The farther you run
The less chance nobody will know

The sign on the wall says keep out
And that means nobody's allowed in
Stopping to take down the sign
Is like committing a mortal sin

Unconscious Freedom

Everything you have
Was hustled with a smile
Giving up the control
Lasts only a little while

The darkest hour will invade
The sanctity of your spirit
Taking what you have stolen
When it arrives you will hear it

The price has been predetermined
For what you will have to pay
Hesitating for just a moment
You try to find another way

Remember yesterday
That is still alive in your dreams
Tomorrow's crash of utopia
Will rip you apart at the seams

Domination is what you seek to possess
It's the fire in your eye
Exasperated from the efforts
Your unconscious freedom soon will die

The Pulse

The pulse of humanity
Beats with every breath
Regulated with minor infractions
Sleeping in a living death

A sigh of desperation,
A fleeting thought of pleasure
Traveling through the city ruins
The past will live forever

Passionate love cannot exist,
Or has it really ever
Lifetimes of neglect have depleted the emotions
Brought forth this day of never

A kingdom in ruins,
A leader without a following
The pulse of humanity lied
Always to be allowing

A Reason

How can I possibly endure
The endless days of pain?
I need to wash myself clean of you,
Oh, how I need the rain

The sun will rise again
This they tell me is true
But how can I embrace it
Experiencing it without you?

I followed my heart
And it has lead me down this path
Now I'm left to repair the damage alone
From your vengeful wrath

I'm left to cry
Over something I can't even see
Desperate to find a reason,
A reason to let me be

Torn Ends of Sanity

How can you plagiarize my thoughts
Without first entering my mind
You speak only with my words
Leaving your calamity behind

Wrestling with the tortured soul
I can't break free from you in my dreams
Invading the stronghold in desperate search
Is more perplexing than it seems

Leaving has never been a consideration
Separation has lost its appeal
Surrendering your own intentions
I'm your pain when you can't feel

If you took me for a ride inside of your head
Would you still be the same
Or would the trip to insanity
Cause you to continue the game

I run from you with arms wide open
Pretending not to see
The survivor, may he return
When myself is after me

Emotionally Sterile

I want to know that you love me
So please get upset when I don't call
I want you to feel all the emotions of love
So that I know you truly did fall

When you worry about me
It shows that you care
When I can't take your call
I hope you're wondering where?

I need to see the possessive side
Not where you just let things go
I feel safety when you wonder where I am
And not just go "oh"

Love has many emotions
And I want to share them all
I am here for you, *angel*, now and forever
And I want to be there during the times you fall

Where Did You Come From?

I wasn't even looking to fall in love
And I'm sure neither were you
But the more we bonded
The more we realized we have a love so true

True love always happens
When you're not looking or wanting it gone
But real, honest love happens maybe once in a life
And when it comes you don't want it to go wrong

When you find your missing piece
You can't lie to yourself that you're happy when you're not
When all you can think about
Is the one you've dreamt about and now you got

Love isn't about timing
Love is about being happy with your choice
True love gives you the options
Because love has a voice

Seven Steps to Freedom

The time is right
And that you can believe
With the day of reckoning fast approaching
On this summer's eve

The ominous clouds roll in
And suffocate the morning sky
Lightning bolts crash to the ground
Without as much as a sigh

Tears of crimson glide down the face
Of a non-existent little child
Feeling despondent for not trusting
The love for desperation grows wild

Opportunity to reconcile
Has been cast out to sea
Caught in the riptide
Drifting away from reality

Seven steps to freedom
Shimmer aboard the coast
Consumed by the horizon
The everlasting fire is the host

Back Again

Sometimes when I look back
It scares me what I see
I allowed you to control everything
And lost is the person who is me

You crept under my defenses
Penetrating with striking force
You removed my inner workings
Without any sign of remorse

You showered me with gifts
That someone else had bought
Everything you didn't do
Was given careful thought

Stripped of the man I used to be
Living without my pride
It's time to recapture what was stolen,
I refuse to be denied

The Wall

Manipulating my feelings for your amusement
Left me vulnerable and unguarded
You professed your undying love to me
And my heart you bombarded

I fell for you when I wasn't looking
Or even wanting to find love
But we were given a thousand signs
Like it was an order from God above

We got swept up in our love
And each other is all we could think about
We knew it, we felt it
That our love had no doubt

Then out of the blue
You slammed the door in my face
You said there's no room for my love
That it should find another place

I started the next day
To reconstruct a wall of steel
There will be no getting in
There will be no way to feel

The Friend I Never Had

You know my face
Yet my name you don't remember
You say you've known me for a day
But it's been from January to December

You know where I live
Yet you don't know the color of my home
You tell me that you've been sheltered lately
Living in a dome

You say that you know me
That we are best friends
I am a complex and misunderstood person
How do we even blend?

My favorite color is blue
Yet you insist that it's red
You may know my face
But to you my name is dead

No Easy Answer

Losing a friend can be the hardest thing
When there is no logical reason
Struck down in the prime of life
Never to live another season

It leaves a void that cannot be filled
No matter how many years go by
Reliving old memories through pictures
Leaves you asking the question "why?"

Others cannot grasp the magnitude
Of the impact your loss has felt
It's almost as if someone has ripped out your heart
And beat it with a belt

No two people share the same emotions
When it comes to a friend's untimely death
That's why it's so important to live life to the fullest
Until you take your final breath

Love's Repression

If I were to tell you I love you
Would you believe that it grew overnight?
If I were to tell you it's never ending
And my love has no end in sight

If I were to tell you that I gave you my heart and soul
And that you were the only person with the key
If I were to tell you that my love would see us through the end
Would you believe my soul can be seen
with a gaze only you can see?

I will tell you the answer is yes
The dream life you want awaits you
My love for you is so strong and real
It's the kind of love you know is true

We connect on every level
And our hearts and souls form as one
For every man and every woman there is but one connection
And you're lucky if your search is ever done

I love your perfections and your flaws
I love you for who you are and what you'll become
You are a gift sent from the heavens
And no more will your heart grow lonesome

A Flower Blossoms

Love is always being there
Even when your body can't
Love is being there unconditionally
Without having to go off into a rant

Love is realizing there is no limit
Or even an end
Love is understanding that miles are nothing
And true undying love you can send

Love is patient, waiting and hoping
For that magical day to come
Love is not for the weak
Those who want their piece and then some

Love is watching it develop over time
Growing stronger with the passing of each day
Love is sharing the good times and the bad
And crying together as you finally find your way

Sign of the Times

Stop the screams, stop the insanity
Stop the voices crying in my head
What do I have to do to make you leave
What more needs to be said

The silent shivers fill my body
Corrupting the powerful persuasion
Exclamation points subdue the question marks
Allowing for a peaceful invasion

I do everything you ask
And never once have you begged
I've fulfilled your every desire
My ambition you have pegged

Why have you chosen me
To invade and control
All I want is for you to leave
Because love has taken its toll

You are an unwanted guest
Living where you o not belong
Existing for my destruction
Replacing right with wrong

Roll of the Dice

Extinction preserves life
As it devours death
The stranglehold captures finality
From the fossil's breath

Glaciers remain a fugitive
Adrift from society's laws
Excavating the intentions
Reveals nature's flaws

Voluntary destruction
Is a crisp, decisive slice
Seasoned for the appetite
It's a flavor without a spice

Victory is shallow,
Empty and wasted
It's spoiled in appearance
And should never be tasted

Bloodline Cast

I was born the prince of fools,
Seated a long side of the king
The golden boy in the golden palace
Given a key without a ring

Everything was always given
Although nothing ever shared
The serpent of the vine hardened my heart
Without even being prepared

An heir to a fortune,
Cursed from tradition
I am prepared for the blessing,
Given with repetition

The bondage of today
Will set me free from the past
Determined to ensure longevity
From the bloodline cast

The Mask

Don't waste your outrage on me
It's time for you to take the blame
The collapse of your own morality
Can be called but by only one name

Sensitive to absolutely nothing
Fighting back the fallen tears
The climax to termination rolls on
With the onslaught of the forgotten years

Begging for safety and comfort,
A haven in which you can call your own
Burdened by the weight of a feather
You flock to the shores alone

Transporting the fever to the living
Reinforces the call of the wild
Determined to battle for a cause unknown
Incinerates the love of a helpless child

Fatal Epidemic

There is nothing I'd like more
Than to crush your head with one firm blow
Watching you beg for mercy
Only feeds my power to grow

Playing God is a symbolic gesture
Healing the dormant gene
Stranded in the crossfire unprotected
The ruptured vein cannot be seen

Blind to the vicious attack
Soon to be released
The common addiction we share
Is the tempest of the deceased

I dance for them
Like a puppet on a string
Swallowing the hallucinogen
With a vial of blood from the king

The child has been driven out,
Destroyed to meet the demands
Security is a fabricated inspiration
When the decisions are not in my hands

Carousel

I will keep you inside of me
When it's time to go away
The tragedy of a lonely spirit
Has been lifted, today

The emperor of freedom
Has called for my return
Wallowing in the decade of secrecy
My title is unjustly earned

Cold blue rolling hills
Disappear into the sea around
Guarding rumors of paradise
Tempting fate with a holler's sound

Brief glimmers of hope
Befall the stars of the spurned
Brittle is the holiday remembered
Victory is the veil burned

Loneliness

Loneliness is a privilege,
Not a punishment or a crime
The sanctity of one's soul rejuvenates
Alone, at the passing of time

Overcrowding segments
Influence the motion of success
Trapped inside the naked union
Trimmed with acrid bitterness

The beauty of sorrow
Is the reflection that it bares
It can never be appreciated
If it always must be shared

Truth is the only witness
In the closet of the mind
Searched by many who came looking
But they will never find

Searching

My child, what you have asked me
Has caught me totally off guard
I don't want to give you a quick response
I'll have to think real hard

I feel such a failure
Because the answer is right there
It will take some time for me to find it
Please don't think that I don't care

Why can't you ask me something easy?
An answer I could give you right now
This is obliquely complicated
You have no idea just how

I don't want to lead you astray
Or ever let you down
Your beautiful smile should always be seen
And not the lonely frown

I will do my best to find the answer
Because even I do not know
When it becomes apparent
Together we shall grow

Game Over

Take a deep breath and relax
You know this is something that must be done
The game has gone on much too long
And it's impossible that it can be won

A lot of thought has been given
The options were heavily weighed
There is no way to rectify the damage
My welcome has been overstayed

The tears I cry every night
Burn from the depths of my soul
I'm tired of being scared and lonely
And falling short of my every goal

It seems the harder I fight, the further I fall
And everything I do is wrong
I cannot dance to the music anymore
The tune that's playing is an unfamiliar song

It's time for the rebirth
To see what's on the other side
Plunging into the new world below
The new beginning will be my guide

Broken Crutch

Tonight is the night to fight the pain
Tomorrow is for healing
Numb from an overdose of insecurity
Nailed to the cross of feeling

Refusing to accept the possibilities
That somehow you exist
Walking alone through the desert
A cool drink you cannot resist

Suffocating my spirit
Plays only a small role
My internal craving to flourish
Is what you seek to control

Torn apart at the seams
Waiting for you to call
I see you standing in the doorway
Anticipating me to fall

Emptiness is fooling me
Into creating a false submission
Guided by precise neglect
Time for the closing benediction

A Man of War

No longer an entity
A creation or a product of the living
The complexities of the internal program
Eliminate the need for forgiving

Once thought of as an intellect, a humorist
Of a mind on the rise
They were frightened by the unknown
And with it, all of the ties

Consequences for their actions do not exist
For their silence could be bought
With electronic genetics implemented
The magic new dimension is what they sought

Though truly sensitive by nature
Exorcising the demon gleam
He's a man of war for their desires
Whose silence is louder than a scream

Trilogy

Punish me one more time
To ease your aching heart
Settle down the ocean of darkness
So the waters, they may part

Kill me again
If you feel it necessary to survive
Death will overcompensate the inadequacies
Keeping me from coming alive

You do not intimidate me
O' mistress of the light
I will allow you to succeed
If you vacate the recesses of the night

Pillow talk is lonely
When there is one to a crowd
Preference is to be admired
To cry myself asleep, aloud

Chess

You captured my pawn as I expected
Not a wise choice on your part
You're walking into my snare
Set up right from the start

It's become quite the battle between us
Your style is incredibly unique
The board you have is gorgeous
And the chiseled pieces can almost speak

Eerily silent
Your moves are nothing less than grand
But I have a great counter move,
Something I have planned

It's been quite some time since we locked horns,
Our matches I never forget
Even though I have yet to get the upper hand
Losing to you I never regret

The Midnight Run

Today is the day
When tomorrow comes alive
Fighting back the quiet tears
Soon the lonely hour will arrive

Memories have corrupted the picture
Cast upon an empty screen
Shoplifting storefront visions
Releases a side seldom seen

Believing if only for a moment
That courage can strike without reason
The new year lives in a day
Embracing the exhausted season

Intensity and passion
Collaborate to provide the wealth
But the slayer from the hollows
Plots to invade liberties health

Lying down in a bed of roses
Seizing the minutes of the second
The call from the unknown will be answered
When the midnight run is beckoned

-Red IV

The veins in my head are bulging
As the sweat rolls down my face
My teeth are clenched so tight
It feels like they're moving out of place

The fire beneath my breath smolders
As catastrophic thoughts emerge
My chest is pounding like a drum,
I hope that I can resist the urge

Dignity is for the weak
And pain is the all-power
Standing toe-to-toe- with pride
Never shall I cower

Falling down is simplistic
Rising meets the demands
Peace and goodwill do not exist
In these blood-stained hands

The rush of adrenaline is persuasive
Coaxing the danger from within
The primal needs are activated
Time for the –red to begin

What Is

A decade of disaster
Entombed in a life of despair
The misgivings of tomorrow await
On a daybreak's lonely glare

The cycle is vicious,
Unrelenting and unforgiving
Sleep keeps me awake
While death keeps me living

The ocean of darkness sparkles
As morning turns into night
With it the demons of fear rumble
From beneath the shelter of white

Distinguishing characteristics
Have blended into one solid form
Dazed and confused I wander
Trying to weather a mother's storm

Courting the Militia

The conflict is hardly even fair
Being unarmed and unprotected
I have fought hard to stay afloat
But the espionage could not have been detected

You were supposed to be my ally
Except your actions tell another tale
Using the weapons at your disposal
How can I do anything but fail

You obliterated my defenses
And penetrated vital forces
Thieving valuable energy
Then distributing it to the rival forces

It's not your war
Despite the bloodshed on your ground
Victory is but a silent passing
When tempting fate of the hell-bound

Neutrality remains a mystery
Funding your own purpose at any cost
By choosing to enter the conflict
Nothing gained will be everything lost

The Call

Your picture is all I dream of
Existing without a flaw
Parading through my memory
The image is vainly raw

Passing through the gateway
Inside the shattered glass
All too soon you'll arrive
And leave at a moment pass

You are easily misunderstood
With motives forever hidden
Perched upon the window sill
The time is all but written

Being the king of wind and flame
You feast upon the fallen steer
Captivity in an emerald case
Awaits through the broken mirror

From Behind the Wall

I love you, I adore you, and I need you
But you scare me half to death
Whenever I am near you, I tremble
Deep down I have to hold my breath

I can never let anyone see
What it is that only I know
I have to keep my defenses up
And put on a real good show

It's therapeutic in a way
Keeping you close by my side
What a better way to prepare myself
The terror you cannot hide

The forces of nature are working with me
Though my instincts tell me to run
It's a battle of ultimate proportions
For me it can never be won

Ten Years Gone

As I retire for the evening
With my whiskey and a book
I pause to absorb my surroundings
And take another look

Who would have thought
Life would be like this
Broken and beaten down
I will never miss

A soft cry emerges
From the nursery down the hall
I scamper to my little darling
But I run into a wall

Surrounded by bricks and mortar
The door, I cannot find
The cries are becoming more prominent
I am going out of my mind

Where is my darling?
Where could my baby be?
Barricaded somewhere deep inside
Crying to be free

Slipping Away

Chauffeured to the brink of insanity
By a driver without a car
Entering the state of oblivion
Alone, you have come so far

Gone is everything you ever learned
Everything that was ever taught
You chose to ignore the paved road
Instead, the rocky terrain is what you sought

Peace and comfort come to you
In forms not seen by others
Hostility is your friend
Where confusion and fear are your brothers

It's a choice you didn't make
But one that was freely received
Binging on the enemy is the only way
To no longer feel you've been deceived

Universal

Shocked into humiliation
Sympathy violates the scorned
Reluctantly he bows his head in defeat
Knowing he will not be mourned

Erased from the memories
Of the ones he loved the most
He must now accept his role
As living life as a ghost

Exiled by the kiss of fate
He now resides in a place newly created
Conditions are almost uninhabitable
And unity has become outdated

It's a society of one
Where anguish is the only neighbor
Illustrated by the puppet masters
Who are reaping the fruits of their labor

Sweeping aside the sorrow
And cleansing the body of pain
He must combat the fear from within
Eternally festered it shall remain

Where Do I Go?

If you cannot love me
Then what shall I do?
The gift of your heart was everything
It was all that I knew

I failed in so many ways
That I dare not come back
I lied to myself for trusting
That truth is the right track

I opened my heart to you,
Wanting you to explore
Then you took away its contents
And abruptly slammed the door

You left me shattered and ruined
But he blame must be shared
I allowed you to have access,
I was the one who dared

My last breath was a memory
Of how it felt to die
You gave me life in an instant,
And your love in a lie

The Battle Rages On

Thirteen progressive cries
Each with its own personal connotation
Give credence to their meager existence
Desperate for affirmation

The elders maintain their perspective positions
Protruding in the darkness from their perch
Connected by a blanket of white
Their failure will cause a search

Pillars of soft flakes cleanse their soul
A sign of determination and virility
The thousand soldiers who are standing guard
Are proud of their ability

Smoky lenses materialize within the regime
A fixture of profound success
Order and stability are still in control
Only one problem to address

Out in the distance a foreigner remains
Unable to conform to the golden rules
He was once an outstanding member of theirs
Until he was forced into a bitter duel

Chastised for his new appearance
He was cast out to protect the group
The matriarch who sentenced him to banishment
Tried to keep him in the loop

Keep the Faith

One more injection
And the process will be complete
Quivering with anticipation
The aroma of success is bittersweet

The plunger is fully loaded
And the arm has been wrapped
Time to say good-bye to destinies face
Through the vein that's been tapped

The fuel that is expelled intermittently
Is to help reignite the fire
While the priest prepares to give the last rights
Behind the voice in the choir

Death is a cloak for extermination
That awakens a shift in time
There is no other viable passage
To alleviate the stress of Satan's crime

Judging the honor
And befriending the rise of the fall
The perpetual motion is highly coveted
Always fearing safety's call

Dream Warrior

Give my regards to nobody
As if anybody really cares
I will not kiss you good night
Or keep you in my prayers

You have become a self-righteous servant
Performing in the theater of the absurd
Confiscating the hatchlings
Then disposing all traces of the bird

Grinding away at the metal
That has encompassed your lair
No time to alert the lion
No time to wake the slayer

It is no longer about love
Nor is it about respect
Ignorant to the world around you
And the arrogance you protect

I'm Coming Home

I don't want to break away
Before it's too soon
Disembodied even momentarily
Like the seed from a mother's womb

Recapturing the youth from today
Obliges the impure
United against the compulsion
Braving the new frontier

Drowning in a waterless ocean
The lifeline is still in sight
Dangling just out of arms reach
It must be grasped outright

A token gesture is made
Sentiments that are deceiving
Brought upon by an empty heart
That has you unjustly believing

Your words are intricately woven
Structured for success
The cross you carry is radiant
With the halo you deftly caress

The Regime

A victim of authority
Drunk from the devil's hate
Patriotic to the outcropping
Freelancing the collector's gate

Homegrown insanity,
Deep rooted and heavily protected
Vulnerable to the flash of a comet,
Nightfall has become infected

Stability comes in a bottle
And peace on a crystal mirror
The leverage of the hand vanishes,
Reality couldn't be clearer

Wed to prophet
Until death do part
The capacity to breathe
Has been nurtured from the fallen heart

Spiral Genocide

Why are you still haunting me
After you left so long ago
I didn't deserve your kind of love
My identity was finally starting to show

Your affection is crippling
Driving me into your web of deception
We are soul mates of another existence
Married to a dream without a reception

Being with you is addictive
A drug I can do without
I struggle to fight off your advances
But your false security removes any doubt

I hate what you do to me
For invading my inner being
Can't you feel the pain you are causing?
Can't you look at what I am seeing?

I must get over you
To allow myself to survive
Each day that passes I am alone
Is one more day I am alive

Paradise Lost

You have a morbid sense of belonging
That derives from a warped and twisted mind
The frail appearance you perceive is deceptive
Your character cannot be easily defined

Manipulation is a curious diagnosis
But then you already knew the signs
You let your weakness overtake you
Crossing over the crimson line

You are the only one who cannot be convinced
That the tide always turns in your favor
Relishing in the thoughtless destruction
The horrid aftermath is what you savor

Living on a belief system that you created
Purifies your shallow existence
The final destination of your soul has been mandated,
You have won with little resistance

Breathe

Caught in the trap
With nowhere to run and nowhere to hide
Nothing can stop the inevitable
The purpose shall be denied

Randomly searching for the release
To detach from the chains
Bound together for an eternity
The unholy matrimony remains

The sheep wander aimlessly
Like a shepherd without a flock
Time has been erased
As the hands are removed from the clock

There is no sign of the dead
Having been removed from the plan
Embrace the voice that cries out
From the illegitimate son of man

Carousel

I will keep you inside of me
When it's time to go away
The tragedy of a lonely spirit
Has been lifter, finally on this day

The emperor of freedom
Has called for my return
Wallowing in the decade of secrecy
My title is unjustly earned

Cold blue rolling hills
Disappear into the sea around
Guarding rumors of paradise
Tempting fate with a hollers sound

Brief glimmers of hope
Befall the stars of the spurned
Brittle is the holiday remembered
Victory is the veil burned

One-Way Street

You cannot possibly believe
The fabrication that easily flows
They are your words, your thoughts
Yet I am the only one who knows

You have been trapped for so long
Living your life in deceit
The brave soldier you are
You were feeding off your conceit

The mirror cannot lie
But for you hides the reflection
Can't you see the flawed exterior
Or is it all a misconception

The farther you float away
The more difficult you'll be to retrieve
Severing your lifeline in haste
To live in the land of make-believe

Truth is always with you
It's a fact you cannot deny
The time has come to face reality
And your real self you must identify

The Day of the Dog

Always on the prowl
Searching for victims to devour
Death ravages the soul unexplored
Frozen impressions are given the power

Blood drips from the snout
After feeding on another fresh kill
Transformed into the day of darkness
Eclipsing expectations at will

On the run from a lawless society
Existing on the misfortunes of others
Packed tightly within the chosen ones
Those who are now considered brothers

Harboring destiny's secret
The price for allegiance is learned
Conscious of the scent that lingers
The languid cannot be discerned

Time

Time is the essence
Of all of life's travels
Stealing precious moments
As they begin to unravel

Quietly the sand falls through the glass,
One grain at a time
Never to be seen again
Only to be relived in the mind

A whisper in the wind
Flow like a gentle river
Passive are the damns built up
Rebellious to the day's giver

Measured in fragments
So that the mind can grasp
Time is but a chain to be worn
That has but one clasp

Mount Fury

Walking along side the wretched
The chivalrous has become disdained
Misguided by the Polaris
The search must be maintained

Desperation breathes new life
Into a vacant and meaningless existence
Hitching a ride on the heavens
The faltering beacon slices with little resistance

Playing the game of eternity
With rules not easily defined
The travels of destiny's secret
Is only available to the blind

There is no time to deny
For the unforgiven cannot wait
The archaic boundaries have been violated
Re-defining the path to the gate

Romancing the bride of rejection
Escalates satisfaction to an all new high
Scripted from the author of lucidity
The anomaly instructs paradise from the vacant sky

Borrowed

I believed everything you say
In spite of what I hear
You torture me with your love
Whenever you are near

Silent and broken
My spirit has been driven
Of myself I am yours,
Always have I given

The cloud that engulfs me
Is yours and yours alone
Molded to suit your needs
Delicately, my clone

I don't fear the stillness
Instead, embrace its sorrow
I follow the silence to you
With dreams of our tomorrow

Indifference

You don't fit in or belong
In any place or time
Suspended in nonexistence
Living past your prime

Exposing yourself to the masses
Would prove a great mistake indeed
Your insistence to reveal your identity
Is based on nothing short of greed

Imprisoned for an eternity
For attempting an unsuccessful escape
Withdrawing the shroud of agony
Over you in victory it is draped

You must now live in relative obscurity
For freedom is only a passing thought
Forget everything you have ever learned
For the new education cannot be fought

Tick Tock

The silence of the laughter
Has masked the years of pain
Continued torture from the mob
Drives the man insane

Fighting back the tears
Trying to keep the mental edge
Provoking the passive plane
With curiosity it's alleged

Threatening to destroy
By the implosion from within
Arrogance cannot destroy
The fury set to begin

Everything that has been done
Is unlike anything before
Vanished is the radiance
Welcomed is the horror

No Wonder

Will miracles ever cease to amaze
Those who want to believe
Or will havoc reign
Without any reprieve

Claiming to be
Something that does not exist
Being true to yourself
You cannot resist

The picture you paint
Deceives even the harshest critic
Contrast in colors is vital
Leaving the observers paralytic

Applause to you
And your charade
Far be it from me
To rain on your parade

Free Falling

I cringe at the thought
So foreign yet so familiar
My temperature escalates beyond the limits
All the while the room grows chillier

Blatantly sadistic
The punishment is well received
I tried to be apprehensive
But I allowed myself to be deceived

Are you unforgiven too
For stepping out into the rain
Calling for a rainbow of fire
To help alleviate the pain

My own miracle
Was willed unto thee
Experience paints a hazy picture
Of an intimate union of certainty

Rise of the Fall

As sure as the sun rules the day
And the stars and moon rule the night
Scorching winds will engulf the evil
Leaving the pure to hold the light

The biblical truth
Is just a proverb away
Mortality is the sweetest revenge
To keep the unworthy at bay

The last rights of freedom
Are whispered inside a holler
Prepare for the everlasting reign
From the truth of the collar

It is not yours
Nor is it mine
We're living on borrowed land,
Living on borrowed time

Eating the fruits
Of somebody else's labor
Go onward to live again
And call upon your neighbor

Left Behind

The blood-stained pillow
Holds the impression of a nightmare come true
Fantasies of futures past
Come alive with horrifying vengeance anew

Fibers easily overlooked
Are quickly swept under the bed
Forces of nature turn
The path of freedom has been misled

Chronicled in the report
From the powers that be
Slighted by the event
Claiming to see

Brushed aside
Like a rebel hair dangling down a face
The pillow has been removed
Vanished without a trace

Firestorm

You left me stranded
For the last lonely minute
Gone to roam the seas eternally without purpose
Absorbing the life that dwells within it

Rolling up the sleeves of depression
Vital to the proper upbringing
Dancing to music that's never heard
And voices that are never singing

What used to be insignificant
Has turned into a malignant growth
Crying at the loss of one,
Celebrating the harvest of both

Speak to me
If only for a second in time
Take the elevator down to the lobby
And kiss me before I climb

I am weak from the journey,
Bought with my very soul
Flailing my arms in desperation
Never to gain control

Razor's Edge

A natural-born intimidator
With a hunger for disaster
Breeding to sanctify your insecurities
Demanding to be the master

You claim to be the chosen one
With actions defined in every breath
Lifting the shadows from the image
You hide behind the mask of death

The love you portray is a smoke screen
Succumbing to the pressures of a timeless force
Ejecting the potential of a silent embrace
The rage within is all you can endorse

It's a parallel universe you conceived
Catered to your every whim
Fused together in harmony
The margin of failure is slim

Almost There

Winning the lottery
Temporarily fills a void in your life
Buying a new truck
Only causes headache and strife

Owning a house
Doesn't always make a home
Sometimes you feel you don't fit in
Sometimes you're alone

Monetary things can always be replaced
But what's inside of you can't
A heart without love dies
Just like watering a plant

Everything in life can be replaced
Because they are all just stuff
Giving up everything to follow your heart
Is actually not that tough

I Believed

I believed in fairytale endings
That dreams do come true
I believed in true love
After I fell in love with you

I am a romantic at heart
And treat my love like she's the best
When it comes to loving her
My heart does not rest

I wanted to be her knight
And sweep her off her feet
We made an instant connection
On the day we did meet

My love cannot be returned
And there's nobody here to blame
I fell for the woman she is
And nothing will be the same

My love pushed her away
And no longer did she want to be with me
I believed in happy endings, her and I
She did too but not with me

The Invisible Architect

Shielded by titanium
The workers built a massive sight
It was the unseen eighth wonder of the world
And it was constructed air tight

The blueprint was designed
And developed from a need to survive
Although no visitors are allowed to marvel it
It is something that's been brought to life

Its sheer beauty and raw design
Will leave a selected few in awe
The security that protects it is harsh
Making it punishable under law

You cannot climb it, you cannot see it
But you know that it is there
You may be encouraged to penetrate it
But you're only living in your own nightmare

Real Love

Real love exists
And not the kind you're used to
Being in love and having love
Is a whole separate issue

Loving someone is easy
But being in love is meant to stay
Saying "I love you" without the emotion is simple
When being in love takes your breath away

Real love is supportive and nurturing
Kind words to build self-esteem
Nothing is more gratifying
Than to stare into your eyes and watch them gleam

I will never speak a harsh word
Or make you feel out of place
My real love
Only wants to see that beautiful smile on your face

Pampered

If you were by my side
I would take care of you best that I can
I would love you endlessly
And show you daily that I'm your man

You work too hard
And that much is true
I would take that burden away
And give my *angel* time for you

You need to be spoiled
Without any expectations in return
Your loyalty and trust is all I ask
And there is nothing for you to earn

Time together without others near
Is exactly what we need to keep our love alive
A relationship built on a neighborhood
Makes it hard to survive

The Game of Love

I followed every rule
And lived by my guide
I ran from love as far as possible
And still there's nowhere to hide

I used every trick I know
Except changing my name
Love is nothing to play with
Love is a nasty game

It doesn't matter who you are
Or the nice things you've done
In the game of love
It showed me that it cannot be won

You can love somebody
With all of your heart and soul
But love is the master of the game
Leaving nothing but an empty hole

I'm taking my game pieces
And trying a different game
Love has cornered the monopoly
And I don't want the outcome the same

When Was the Last Time?

When was the last time
You got a passionate kiss for no apparent reason?
When was the last time
You received a bouquet of flowers, even out of season?

When was the last time
You came home and were queen for the night?
When was the last time
You didn't give in just to stop a fight?

When was the last time
When all you wanted was to be held oh, so tight?
When was the last time
It wasn't thought this meant sex all night?

When was the last time
You tried to talk about your day?
When was the last time
Someone didn't look away?

There will never be a last time
Because you have yet to experience a love so real
There will never be a last time
If you allow yourself to feel

The Looking Glass

I admire your failures
Although painful and discouraging
The character you have attained
Can be summed up as encouraging

Do not let a day go by
Without looking at how far you came
Some things will always be different
And nothing will be the same

Printed in Great Britain
by Amazon